T0105808

Ocean Inspirations

thoughts upon the water

Inspirations for Weathering Life's Storms

Dwainia W. Tullis

It isn't often that we meet someone who is so willing to share and enlighten us without expecting monetary gain. I have found Dwainia to be such a person. With her gracious spirit and attentiveness she glides you through your own thoughts but on a more spiritual level allowing you to visualize the solution as if the outcome came from within you. But you needed a little push to release (bring it out). You now grow into a better awareness of yourself.

Let yourself be guided into an awakening of what lies beneath the surface of your own spirit. (Heart)
-Linda M. Wyatt retired Port of Los Angeles Police Dispatcher

Order this book online at www.trafford.com
or email orders@trafford.com

Most Trafford titles are also available at major online book retailers.

© Copyright 2010 Dwainia W. Tullis.
All rights reserved. No part of this publication may be reproduced, stored in a retrieval system, or
transmitted, in any form or by any means, electronic, mechanical, photocopying, recording, or
otherwise, without the written prior permission of the author or the photographers.

Printed in Victoria, BC, Canada.

ISBN: 978-1-4269-2661-7

*Our mission is to efficiently provide the world's finest, most comprehensive book publishing
service, enabling every author to experience success. To find out how to publish your book, your
way, and have it available worldwide, visit us online at www.trafford.com*

Trafford rev. 3/05/2010

 www.trafford.com

North America & international
toll-free: 1 888 232 4444 (USA & Canada)
phone: 250 383 6864 ♦ fax: 812 355 4082

Ocean Inspirations

Photo by Samuel Brown

To my father and mother for being the greatest inspirations in my life. My father wanted to be the first to have a copy of this book. He passed away March 4, 2009; so this book is dedicated to him and my mother shall be the first to receive a copy of this book.

Thank you Mom and Dad.

About the Book

Engaging OCEAN INSPIRATIONS is a journey of change and transformation.
Prepare yourself for the journey!

Remember still waters DO run deep. OCEAN INSPIRATIONS presents an opportunity for deep introspection. The book inspires you to go within to find the best part of you that is hidden.

Here is a work to help you get to that tender part of yourself where you can bring to the surface, get more light, grow and blossom into that wonderful Being of Light that you are! Growing and blossoming is the journey of our lives.

Presented are inspirations to encourage and guide you along the pathway, we call Life.
Learning to 'BE' is one of the greatest challenges of a lifetime and our thoughts are what guide our steps. So be mindful of your thoughts. Guard your thoughts like precious jewels, for precious jewels they are; along the pathway.

ENJOY THE JOURNEY!

About the Author

Having resided in Missouri, Illinois, Delaware, Labrador and California, Dwainia's life journey has made her accept and embrace change.

Throughout her journey Dwainia has had to transform herself. Through observation of the natural flow of life, she has accomplished the 'Art of Transformation', which is change that this book reveals.

Photo by Samuel Brown

The Writings of Ngozi Winif

Presented by Dwainia W. Tullis

The inspirations that follow are messages received from the realm of the Angels to bring understanding and peace to mankind.

From the PURE LOVE MEDITATION sessions year 2008

Caption: Photo by Samuel Brown

Acknowledgements

I would like to give a special thank you to my girlfriend/sister, Wendy in Waukegan for all the love and support she has given me in every area of my life since we were teens. Our lives have paralleled since we met.

And to my daughter Winnetka for putting up with me in my frenzied work days, sorting out what I need without knowing exactly what I need. Thank you, Winnetka.

And for all of my clients/friends who listened to me as I shared newfound knowledge, whether they understood or accepted. I appreciate you all. Thank you so much for the support.

Contents

OPENNESS - Photo by Dwainia Tullis

Openness

Openness is the beginning.

POWER is all around

The OCEAN, the LIGHT, the WIND,

Hear the Power.

Feel the Power.

Know the Power.

Now see!

Look and see.

The Omnipresent,

The Omnipotent,

The Omniscient

POWER WE CALL GOD!

CHANGE - Photo by Samuel Brown

Change

CHANGE is all around.

At times it is in small doses and easy to absorb.

And at times the CHANGE is so enormous,

we feel broken down.

Nonetheless it is all CHANGE.

Embrace this thing called CHANGE,

for it is;

really is your saving grace.

For without it, we would not be…

Embrace CHANGE.

As rock is to sand and is to the ocean,

it is touched, shifted, and moved.

The landscape displays its majestic beauty.

Change is what causes that beauty.

Change is life and love.

Embrace we must, for Change is.

Embrace the Art of Change.

Watch to learn.

Nature teaches.

Watch to learn.

Change.

Photo by Samuel Brown

At the Altar

This night release and forgiveness has been given and shed.
A new freedom is here within,
freedom from the bonds of insecurity fear incapacities and
faults.
Decisions made have been made.
So be it. Release it!

Self has forgiven self.
What a peace!
Self has aligned with
The Angelic and Heavenly Beings.

One, we are, and one we have always been. This is the way of
the Most High God.

There is no nor has there been any separation from God.
All is illusion.

Our existence is to pass through realms to realize…
The connection has never been lost.
It is the fog, the very thick fog that clouds our vision, which has
created the illusion of separation.

As we meditate, still our minds, speak to the Above,
the sun shines, dissolves the vapors of fog from our visions and
we see!! How comforting.

Yet there is more. Our ears are cleansed. And as we speak to
the Above, we hear! We hear and know the Above and the
Heavenly Host of Angelic Beings.

So now! The moment has arrived.
Forgiving of the self to the self from the self is freedom itself.
Then, we hear more clearly the Heavenly Host.

Confidence is exalted. Requests are made known, and you know they have been heard and you have heard the response. Forward.

Confidence is no longer a question of how or will I; it is understood with great strength and magnitude.
One's ability is united and aligned with the Most High, the Above, the Heavenly Host.

Scales are removed from the eyes, wax removed from the ears and gripping released from the heart.

One becomes as air, freedom of movement, lightweight, moving and never seen.

Peace enters in, immeasurable peace.

Time no longer has bars to hold you, for wind is not held, it moves!

The Heavenly Host, The Above, The Most High have spoken.

PEACE.

NEVER TO LATE - Photo by Dwainia Tullis

Never Too Late

Never too late, go!

The surprise waits.

Never too late, do what you know to do.

Never too late,

there is always something good that

awaits the recipient, go!

Never say Oh! I am too late!

There waits for the recipient

the Blessing!

It's Never too late.

ALONG THE PATHWAY - Photo by Dwainia Tullis

Along the Pathway

Along the pathway be mindful of your thoughts.

As we walk, we think.

Our thoughts guide our steps,

the steps along the pathway.

Be mindful for there are stones,

loose stones we may not see.

Be mindful you don't slip and fall.

Guard your thought like precious

jewels, for precious jewels they are.

Allow your thoughts to float upward,

clear of weighty things.

Our thoughts carry us to many a place…

Be mindful of your thoughts lest you

Slip and fall along the pathway,

The pathway of life.

PEACE - Photo by Samuel Brown

Peace

Pull down Peace as an apple from a tree.

It's yours for the taking!

Just reach up and take!

THOSE TIMES - Photo by Samuel Brown

Those Times

Those times when aloneness is all around,
we see with earthly eyes people, things and
movements.
Yet aloneness is all around.
We say, why do I feel so alone? And as we search
outward, seeking, looking to connect.
The aloneness grows and what we see appears even
further away.
Paralysis sets in! Oh my! We cry out, internally we
go… a response, a response I hear?
The messengers respond with music, and lyrics, an
awakening, the message!
We feel we begin our route out of aloneness.
The lyrics, the music, the message transports us out
of aloneness .
from the internal to the external we have traveled.
New waves of thoughts, energy and light we find
ourselves engulfed.
Peace is journeys end!
Remember the transport, the travel, and the journey.
Now rest.

VOICE - Photo by Samuel Brown

Voice

Everything has a voice, if we would just listen.

All speak! Do you know the language?

With our hearts we can hear the voice of all things.

Be still, feel your own heartbeat.

Be still, feel your beat with the ocean.

Then, experience the wind, the rocks, the birds and the bugs.

This beat allows us to hear and learn the language of all things.

All things have life, be mindful of this. Let us learn the language of life, the language of life that gives life.

As we live the language of life, we live a more abundant life.

Let all live, and have a more abundant life.

Let us learn the language of life.

For all creation has a language, the language of life.

THE CYCLE OF LIFE - Photo by Samuel Brown

The Cycle of Life

The flowers know they will live again.

In their cell memory it is recorded what they must do.

They grow!

They depend on God (what we call God) to water them, to feed them, to help them sprout out in full blossom knowing the time is allotted for them.

There is a time for every phase of their lives to be lived to the fullest and then they must go.

Go they must, knowing in their cell memory that the seeds they drop will live again.

The flowers live with a complete trust and knowing this will happen again over and over.

They know with no reserve their life.

Be blessed.

SAME GOD - Photo by Samuel Brown

Same God

The same God that causes the flowers to grow

on this side of the world, is the same God who

causes the flowers to grow on the other side

of the world.

DEDICATION - Photo by Dwainia Tullis

Dedication

The sun and the moon are dedicated to themselves, the earth and the people.

The sun's promise of dedication is to give warmth to the earth, life to plants, animals and mankind for growth continual.

The moon's promise of dedication is to give light by night, to assist bringing life into the world and to bring the tide in higher.

Have you found your area of dedication?

What is your area of dedication?

We all have an area!

Once your area of dedication is found, your path to the Most High is made clearer and sight more visible.

Dedicate your life. Clear your path. Create your world exactly the way you have desired.

Dedicate yourself, the way will be shown to you!

DO YOU SAY THANK YOU? - Photo by Samuel Brown

Do You Say Thank You?

Do you say thank you?

You say to whom shall I say thank you?

I say to life, to the life giver, that we call God.

We are awakened from our deep sleep, how dos this happen?

Who, what awakens us?

Oh I woke myself up!

Who or what is myself?

What power does myself have to wake myself?

Where does myself get the power to wake myself?

Begin to speak, morning noon and night.
Speak your thank you, you will be heard and your relationship
begins.

Build your relationship. Develop it, nurture it and watch it grow
and blossom.

Behold a new and magnificent life, full of color, beauty,
fragrance, joy, happiness and most of all Peace.

Bless, Bless, Bless,
AMEN.

CREATION - Photo by Dwainia Tullis

Creation

Who can understand the creation!

How magnificent its beauty and its strength!

Who can blend the array of life as it is with such order?

We call it Nature.
Duplicate, we try. Create?

The rhythms of the ocean waves, the movements of the rocks,
the sounds blended so well together, whom or what has
created such a structure?

The pleasure provided from this creation for each being large
and small is a gift.

Respect that that has created, what we attempt to understand.

Let the creation BE.

By becoming, we become, therefore BE!

As we BE, we return to creation.

Then comes the understanding of the self, others and nature,
therefore creation itself!

RESPECT
BE
And let BE
Then you will see.

SURRENDER - Photo by Samuel Brown

Surrender

Everything unto itself must die, so that the new can come in.

Surrender; as the flower dies it make way for the new flower to blossom bright and beautiful.

PEACE AGAIN - Photo by Samuel Brown

Peace Again

Peace everlasting peace.
Go within to gather peace.

Mix peace with love and most of all gratitude.
Peace will abound.

Always go inward in the inner recesses of our being, the very
essence of our self.

What is self? Self is that that you feel, that tingling, that is you.

Your vibration, your energy is you.
Recognize the differences. Peace abounds.

Go inward to that center and let it spread out from within to
the without.

Go forward!

THE MESSAGE - Photo by Samuel Brown

The Message

The sun rises everyday and it is free!

The air we breathe, the wind we feel is free.

The plant will grow without us and it is free. The food grows without us.

The water is free.

Mankind did not create any of this. How forgetful of us!

Remember, life will happen without us. Look up and say thank you.

There are many parts to the body, the body of life.

Find which part of the body you are and function in that part.

How unaware we can be of our self and how our actions affect our self and others!

If we would just once, step outside of our own shell and look at our actions, how much more we would see, feel and understand.

All feel to a greater or lesser degree.
We know not the mind of the other unless we speak, listen and learn.

DESIRES OF MANKIND - Photo by Dwainia Tullis

Desires of Mankind

Where do they lead, what purpose do they serve?

Is it vanity? What does it do for mankind in its relationship to creation?

To Advance, to Advance to what, when creation is advanced!

Creation in its entirety is advanced already!

Rephrase, rethink, and readjust mankind!

What part of creation are YOU and are you functioning in your natural position in nature as the rest of creation?

Why do you think you are ahead of creation when YOU your self ARE a creation!

Reposition your self, O' man of creation!

THE OCEAN - Photo by Samuel Brown

The Ocean

As the ocean is with water, so is God with us.

It is so!

Speak and think only positive words and thoughts.

The work is in need and we fill a portion of that need.

Let the positive guide us in all we do.

The light shines, so shine!

Go forward children of the light!

Fear no more, for your time is here! NOW! SHINE!

SHINE!

GLOW!

BE LIGHT!

THE LIGHT IS, SO BE!

TALK - Photo by Samuel Brown

Talk

Speak and listen!

You ARE recognized in the Universe.

You are more than a speck!

You are mighty, mighty as the Universe,

and you are as complex as the Universe.

Discovery takes time.

It is the journey of your lifetime, filled with

adventure, hazard, reward and recognition!

LIVE YOUR JOURNEY!

CREATE - Photo by Samuel Brown

Create

Create your environment that you may recognize
you are on and in your journey.

View your life journey from a perspective of
awesome opportunities.

With opportunities come the renewed understanding
of your existence, your growth and your awareness.

Utilize your opportunities as stepping-stones,
getting you closer to those goals and those
utmost desires.

These opportunities are your gifts from the Universe.
Receive them with joy and exhilaration.

Begin to watch yourself blossom
into the wonderful Universe that you are.

Receive your gifts,
get on with your journey
shout thanksgiving to the Universe!

AWARENESS - Photo by Samuel Brown

Awareness

Life presents opportunities and challenges

To be discovered and experienced, then put into use in everyday life.

Recognition, acceptance, realizations and action are sequences to self-awareness.

This new awareness leads to wonderful experiences that bring us into the wonders of creation.

POWER TO BE - Photo by Samuel Brown

Power to Be

Let the Power flow through you like water flowing from a stream.

Let the water, the cleansing healing power of the ocean waves cleanse you as it flows in and heal you as it flows out.

Let the power of the ocean waves, as they hit the shore, go deep, pulling out all the impurities that hide deep within your soul.

Let us rise as the mist of the ocean. Rise into that powerful Spirit Being in human form that we are!

Recognize who and what you are!

Stand up in awareness!

Realize, "I am able".

It is my right by virtue of body and earth to "BE"!

If you are interested in any of the photos featured
in this book, in color or black and white, they may
be purchased from Pure Love Meditation.

You may request size 5x7 or 8x10 framed or unframed.

All inquiries should be sent to purelovemeditation@gmail.com.